Elijah Anointing

Volume 1

The Sound of Abundance of Rain

1 Kings 18:41
And Elijah said unto Ahab, Get thee up, eat and drink; for there is a sound of abundance of rain.

Elijah Anointing

Volume 1

The Sound of Abundance of Rain

Roland Sadoo

Copyright © 2011
Roland Sadoo

All rights reserved. No part of this book may be reproduced in any form without prior written permission from the Publisher.

Published by:

Sharing The Light Ministries
P.O. Box 596
Lithia Springs, GA 30122
www.myholycall.com

ISBN-13: 978-1461191094
ISBN-10: 1461191092

Printed in the United States of America

Scripture Quotations Taken From
The King James Version
(Bold, capitals, and italics added for emphasis)

Book cover design by Sue Morrissey
Sue Morrissey Art & Design
www.suemartist.com

Dedication

I would like to dedicate this first volume to the Father, Son, and Holy Spirit. I thank my God for revealing to me His matchless love and allowing me to share His love and kindness to the world. I also want to thank the Lord for two very special women, with amazing prophetic insight. They made the written recording of this testimony possible. Lois M. Brinkley, who I met shortly after arriving in the United States, is called as a Prophet to the Body of Christ. For more than thirty years, God has used her to prepare the New England area for the end-time Glory of God. C.J. (Cindy) Thomas is the leader and founder of Sharing The Light Ministries. She is currently in the Atlanta area where she and her powerful team of king-priest intercessors, have been praying and interceding more than 15 years for the end-time Glory of God! This three-fold cord that has been established is ordained and confirmed of God. The Lord revealed to Prophet Lois in 1995, that there were many connections to be made. He said: *"The blessings will flow, when the people and things are in place"*. My connection with *"Sharing The Light"* is the beginning of these pieces God has put together. Praise God for His manifold wisdom!

Roland Sadoo

Preface

As I begin to write the introduction to this remarkable testimony by Roland Sadoo, I want to say a few things about God's purpose and destiny for our lives. We all have a perfect destiny in God, but not all have entered into it. This book is a wonderful encouragement to reach higher in God to activate those gifts that He has placed within us at birth.

The Bible is full of the manifold wisdom of God, His story (History), which is His long *"Love Letter"* to His creation. Within the first few pages of this *"Letter",* we are told about the original creation of the earth, its re-creation and the creation of Adam.

He was created to rule and reign on the earth through his love, communion and fellowship with the Lord. We see that the Lord created Adam to have dominion and authority over the earth which he, through his sin and disobedience, lost to the enemy.

But in Genesis 3:15, we are promised our Savior, Jesus Christ, Who would defeat our enemy and restore all that had been stolen from us. We are told that God sent His Son in the fullness of time to redeem us and bring restoration and this is why He was called the *"Last Adam"*.

The Psalmist declares: *Then I said, "Behold, I come; In the scroll of the book it is written of me. I delight to do Your will, O my God, And Your law is within my heart". (Psalms 40:7-8)*

This is reaffirmed in Hebrews, Chapter 10.

Therefore, when He came into the world, He said: "Sacrifice and offering You did not desire, But a body You have prepared for Me. In burnt offerings and sacrifices for sin You had no pleasure. Then I said, 'Behold, I have come -- In the volume of the book it is written of Me -- To do Your will, O God" (Hebrews 10:5-7).

These scriptures confirm that the destiny of Jesus was written in scripture and He knew it. In His earthly life, Jesus found Himself in scripture, meditated upon it and fulfilled it. Our destiny is also written in scripture and Jesus shows us that we are to find ourselves in scripture, meditate upon it and fulfill it!

Not only does God give us shadow pictures in His Word about our Savior; His life, death, resurrection and total dominion, but He also tells our story in beautiful *"patterns and illustrations"*. He gives us these *"concealed"* mysteries about His plan for us, and as His New Testament kings and priests, He gives us the *"honor to search"* them out (Proverbs 25:2).

These patterns and illustrations tell our destiny and purpose; who we are, why we were born and how much we are loved. As we begin to know who we really are, and how we are to touch the world with the love of God, the threads of our lives interconnect to form the most beautiful tapestry!

In the life of Roland Sadoo, we find this principle at work in the most unique way. This man, born and raised in Trinidad, has found his life at different seasons, fulfilling various Biblical patterns and illustrations. It has been prophesied that he is a chosen vessel and he has the mantles of Elijah, Moses, Joseph, David, Solomon, Daniel and others. We see that his life thus far, has mirrored certain elements of their life's character, pattern and devotion to the will and purposes of God.

This man is an extraordinary Prophet who has been gifted to produce a glorious *"change in the atmosphere"* everywhere he goes. He is also uniquely gifted to bring about *"restoration"* through the love and power of our Lord Jesus Christ. He has found himself in scripture, meditated upon it and is fulfilling it!

These glimpses into his life are remarkable, with the promise that God has used him this way in the past; and will continue to use him in even greater ways to facilitate His Glory in these last days.

As you read these *"faith"* stories, your spirit will soar in the joy that these events described could actually happen to him. Your mind will be filled with images of your own success and restoration as you are blessed with the knowledge of how God used him. Also you will realize that you can come to know the voice of God and fulfill His heart's desire for you!

You will be encouraged and challenged to believe God for His unique plan and purpose for your life also! Simple humility and declarations of faith such as; *"God said it, I believe it and it will come to pass"* will begin to propel you into your destiny! Get ready to be *"transformed"* and *"challenged"* as you read this book. Glory to God forever!

C.J. Thomas
Founder & President
Sharing The Light Ministries

Elijah Anointing

Contents – Volume 1

A Glimpse Of Destiny 1

A Change In Direction 5

Prayer For A Farm 13

The Journey For My Farm 21

Prayer For Double Portion 25

Receiving The Double Portion 33

The First Obstacle 37

God's Hands Are Not Tied 41

Roland; Who Is Your God? 47

Bringing Life To The Village 59

The Crippled Man 65

The Donkey Named "Roland" 71

Final Reflections 83

Foreword

This book is a glimpse of the journey of Roland Sadoo, an extraordinary man, called as a Prophet to the Body of Christ. This is only the first volume of many that God will use to bless and encourage His people. As mentioned earlier Brother Roland's life is a tapestry of various kinds of mantles. But his life, mainly, is an illustration of the Prophet Elijah. I believe that as you read this book, you will agree that this is the *"Biblical Pattern"* or *"Illustration"* his life is following.

The cover design is based on 1 Kings, Chapter 18. This is the account of Elijah and the confrontation on Mount Carmel with the prophets of baal. In order to gain a more clear understanding of the events at Mount Carmel, let's go back to the woman at the well in Samaria. Her encounter with the Lord Jesus is found in Chapter 4 of the Gospel of John.

John 4:19-24
The woman saith unto him, Sir, I perceive that thou art a prophet. Our fathers worshipped in this mountain; and ye say, that in Jerusalem is the place where men ought to worship. Jesus

saith unto her, Woman, believe me, the hour cometh, when ye shall neither in this mountain, nor yet at Jerusalem, worship the Father. Ye worship ye know not what: we know what we worship: for salvation is of the Jews. But the hour cometh, and now is, when the true worshippers shall worship the Father in spirit and in truth: for the Father seeketh such to worship him. God is a Spirit: and they that worship him must worship him in spirit and in truth.

This woman was talking about how her fathers worshipped versus the Jewish order of worship. Jesus points out that she and her fathers did not know what they were worshipping! The Jews had the proper order of worship that would bring total deliverance. Jesus also told her that a time would come, *"meaning after His resurrection";* when true worship of the Father would be accomplished in the *"spirit realm"* and not a physical place.

Her ancestors, in the Northern Kingdom, had set up idolatrous worship in the hills of Samaria, at Bethel and Dan, in direct rebellion to worshipping God in the method He has ordained (1 Kings 12:28-33). This idolatry continued to get worse and produced *"drought conditions"* during the time of Elijah.

After more than three years of drought, Elijah called for a showdown at Mount Carmel with the false prophets of baal. Elijah called down *"fire"* from heaven and brought the Israelites back to God (1 Kings 18). The false prophets were killed and the land was purged. After these things Elijah declared; *"There is a Sound of Abundance of Rain"* and then he prayed until the cloud formed (1 Kings 18:41). The Israelites were brought back to *"True Worship"* by Elijah and that produced the *"Rain of God's Blessings"*. What we should embrace here is that Elijah was not just an ordinary prophet. He operated in the authority of a king and priest when he declared the word of the Lord and offered a sacrifice unto Him!

Brother Roland's life is an illustration of how God has used him to *"change the atmosphere"* wherever he goes. He knows how to operate in the power of his New Testament king-priest ministry! He brings people into the knowledge and true worship of our God; the Father, Son, and Holy Spirit. The atmosphere is changed to one of *"transformation and abundance"*, where there was lack or a drought of God's blessings. In this book you will see how God not only transformed individual lives, through him, but entire areas of people. After reading his testimony you will have to agree, that his life is a *"Pattern Illustration"* of Elijah. He is truly a unique *"Gift"* to the Body of Christ for these last days!

Sharing The Light Publications

Chapter One

A Glimpse Of Destiny

"I Will Do The Same For You In America"

My name is Roland Sadoo and I was born and raised in the island of Trinidad. It was not until I came to the United States and to the state of Massachusetts, that I finally understood, why the Lord has taken my life in such an unusual direction.

All those years in Trinidad, I was in training and preparation to be used by God on a larger scale than I could have ever imagined.

It has been more than four years since I have come to America. A couple of years ago, the Lord woke me up at three o'clock in the morning. He came and spoke in a soft voice. He started to talk to me about the extraordinary blessings that He had brought to pass in my life for so many years.

That first morning, when the Lord started speaking to me in *"normal"* conversation; I did not think that much about it, because that's the kind of relationship I have with my Father. The second morning I was again awakened at three o'clock in the morning; and the Lord began again to emphasize the *"unusual"* blessings on my life.

The third morning, at three o'clock in the morning, it happened again and I realized the Lord was really trying to get my attention about something extremely important! I could hear the same voice of the Lord, in my heart, talking to me about my testimony of what He had done for me in Trinidad. He said; *"My son what you did not know was that in Trinidad, beginning thirty years ago, I was preparing you for what I Am going to do with you, in this country, in America. I want you to go to the Churches and share this testimony and let the Believers know; I Am the God of all flesh and nothing is too hard for Me! What I have done for you in Trinidad, I Am going to do for them. This testimony is NOT for the outsiders to the Church or the unbelievers. They can listen to it and partake of some of the blessings. Through which, they will begin to learn how to trust Me and then they will be drawn to Me. But this testimony is for the Believers, the Body of Christ, so that they will know how to trust Me to the fullest!"*

Primarily what the Lord has revealed to my spirit is that these blessings and covenant promises belong to His children! I began to fully realize what God was trying to tell me. These events and blessings were not just the result of my hard work, diligence or even my personal faith. But they were the result of a special gifting that He had placed in me, while I yet in my mother's womb. They were gifts for the Body of Christ in these last days to fulfill His plans and purposes!

God has given me a powerful testimony meant to be shared with the Body of Christ and the world. I have so many testimonies of God's goodness to me! This first volume, I would like to share the events that have shaped my life and destiny; and led me into the Lord's perfect will regarding farming.

Chapter Two

A Change In Direction

Early Life

My parents and grandparents were Catholic and that is the way I was raised in my early life. I attended Catholic school and came to admire a particular priest. He was an Englishman, who would come and minister to us every day. I was about 11-years-old at the time, when I came home and announced to my Mom that I wanted to be a priest! Despite much teasing from my older brother, I kept saying that was what I wanted; to be a priest. Even at that early age, I sensed God calling me into a close, intimate relationship with Him.

About the age of 16, I began to listen to Evangelist Billy Graham on the radio and was drawn by the Holy Spirit to receive Jesus Christ as my Savior and Lord. After high school, I began to visit other churches. I began to hear Christians give their testimonies of what the Lord had done for them. They had a deeper relationship with the Lord than I could understand; and had entered into a level of blessings that I did not have.

I used to leave church and walk or sometimes ride my bike to a beautiful secluded spot, where there was a pond, called Blue Basin. I wanted so much to know my purpose; to know God's plan for my life. I would sit on the bridge there and I would say; *"Lord, how You bless Your children! Are they Your children and am I Your nephew? Lord, I never asked You to make me!"* I repeated that to the Lord many times, but I did not realize what God had in store for me.

"I'm Going To Use You In My Kingdom"

When I was about 19 years old, an American Evangelist came and held a crusade. It was held in a football stadium in Arima, the 3rd largest city. There were thousands of people there. I went with my Mom and a friend. I was sitting in the 7th row, on the 3rd seat. The Evangelist came over and began to point and count to (7) and called to the 3rd person on the right! Everyone was looking at me, figuring out that I was the one he was calling out. I was shocked! He asked me to stand up, and this is the word of the Lord that he spoke over me; *"I see a cloud over you, a dark cloud over you now, but God is going to move that cloud, He is shaking it right now. God is going to use you in His kingdom. God is going to start a work in your life and you will be amazed to see what He will do"*. I could hardly grasp what had just happened! But my Mom and my friend were very excited for me.

After that event, I got affiliated with one large church, and the Lord began to minister to me in my dreams. I was having very unusual dreams and I realized that I had a calling on my life. I never heard a *"voice"*, but mostly I would dream things and I would tell my Mom. She said; *"Probably someday; you just keep pressing on and someday God is going to use you in His kingdom; God is going to use you!"*

The Lord was working in my life in ways that I did not understand. But I got involved in the church and started to pray for people. It was a very large church, and one day Pastor Duncan came over to me and asked; *"Who are you and where are you from?"* I responded to his questions, but always wondered about that encounter.

Sometime after that, there was a woman in the church who had cancer. She needed (3) pints of blood and (2) people had already given. They were asking for someone to go to the hospital and donate a pint of blood. Again, this church was very large with a lot of members and I did not tell anyone I was going. I just got her name and the hospital, and went and donated blood on Saturday. Sunday morning, the Pastor said; *"There is somebody in this church who went to the hospital and gave a pint of blood. Who is it? Would you stand?"* I stood up and he prayed over me and said; *"That is nice, what you did; but the Lord is going to use you in the ministry, He is going to bless you"*. After that everywhere that Pastor Duncan went I was favored to accompany him in his car! I shared things about the gospel with him and he was amazed. I continued to read and study the Bible and began to grow even more, spiritually.

But I still remembered questioning God in those early days sitting on the bridge at Blue Basin. *"God how do You choose other children and bless them financially; You give them all kinds of things and everything else? If they are Your children, then I am Your nephew!"* I would stare at my reflection in the pond and say; *"Lord why are You using other people and not me? Lord I never asked You to make me!"* At that time; I did not understand what the Lord had in store for me. After the prophetic word in the stadium at Arima, the unusual dreams that followed and the prophetic word through Pastor Duncan; I knew the Lord was revealing my destiny. But one of my greatest revelations was yet to come.

Evangelist R.W. Schambach Crusade

In 1973, R.W. Schambach from Tyler, Texas, held a crusade in Trinidad. That single event completely revolutionized my Christian walk and brought me so much closer to the Lord! During that crusade, there was a great outpouring of God's Spirit. I was baptized in the Holy Spirit and spoke in other tongues for (30) minutes! After that I began to walk in a new level of prayer and power. In this new level of prayer, I began operating in deliverance ministry (casting out demons). But more than that, I was infused with God's fervent love for the Body of Christ.

I have continued to develop His love in me. Every time I hear somebody preach or minister the Word, on television or radio, I ask God to bless them. If I read a book, I ask the Lord to bless the author and pray for them. The first thing I do when I enter a church, I pray for the Pastor, the one who is ministering the Word of God. I also pray for world leaders, including every President of the U.S. As I grew in the Lord, I began to understand more about God's love for Israel, His chosen people, and I began to pray for them and constantly bless them. I believe my prayer life and my love for everyone is how God blesses me!

Working For The Government

I got a government job working in the Ministry of Works from 1970 to 1978. I worked in what could be called the *"Payroll department"*. During that time, there were a lot of illegal activities and irregularities in that department.

There were people who had died and their names were never taken off the payroll. The government of Trinidad never knew that these people had, in fact, died and others were using their names to continue to receive salaries. There were also people who had never worked, and yet received salaries in these false or invalid names. The people involved tried to force me to also get involved in these illegal activities and wrongdoings. I decided to give up the job, rather than stay and illegally receive two or three biweekly salaries. So I gave up my job and I prayed a simple prayer. *"Lord, I have given up this job and I believe You are going to take care of me".*

I Have Always Loved Farming

I had an uncle, who is now deceased. At that time he was involved in an agricultural business, pruning of trees, planting flowers and things of that sort. So I began to help him in his business. I would take him to his different job sites and go back for him in the afternoon. One day, while taking him to one of his jobs, from the highway I saw Chicken Pens with chickens flying up and down. I told my uncle that I was going to stop and visit that farm on the way back home. That sparked something in me that day because I have always loved farming and agriculture. I always had a desire to work at it on a large scale, but never had the opportunity.

Chapter Three

Prayer For A Farm

My Prayer For A Farm

As I mentioned earlier, R.W. Schambach had held a meeting in my country. The Lord impacted my life in a powerful way through him. During the meetings, he said, *"Whenever you need something; you have got to be specific with God and tell God exactly what you need"*. I remembered him preaching this, and that word he preached just stayed in my heart and in my soul. After I left my job with the government, I communicated with Brother Schambach's ministry. I decided to write to him a very simple request and said; *"Brother Schambach I want a farm. I have no lands and I have no *money. I have no experience, but I need a farm".* Again it was a very simple letter and I posted it to Tyler, Texas.

It must have been about three weeks later a reply came back from Brother Schambach stating; *"We have prayed in Tyler Texas for your farm. Brother Roland just believe that the farm is on the way. God is going to bring it to pass".* This is the word I was leaning on in faith; that God was going to bring it to pass! I stood believing that He was going to bring my farm.

Visiting The Chicken Farm

On the way home, later that day, I turned into the Chicken farm that I had seen earlier. I spoke to the woman owner and I said to her, *"I see you have chickens here".* She said; *"Yes, we have 'Layers'. We collect eggs and we sell them at the Market place, the malls, different areas, and different places".* I said; *"Well I've given up my job and I would like to sell some eggs".* She said, *"You need to come back tomorrow and see my husband".* The next day I came back to see her husband. I felt led to explain to him everything in regard to my job; all of the irregularities and the wrongdoings. I then told him that I would like to buy eggs from him and sell them at the Market.

He realized how I was wronged; and because of my honesty, I had to give up my job. So he said; *"O.K. I will not cut back on my customers, but we do sell eggs here from home. We only have three thousand chickens. But I will give you some of the eggs to sell".*

He told me to come back on Friday. He said, *"I will give you eggs and you will go to the Market or you could go to the city and sell them. In the city streets the people sell vegetables, dry goods and so forth".* So he gave me the eggs and I went to the city to sell, not realizing some of the problems I would encounter. I had to park my car in the street and display my eggs on top of the car, in order to get customers.

There were others, like myself, who would set up their products in the open market and sell them. The problem was that we were on the street or pavement in front of the vendors with established businesses. We were challenging them for customers and those vendors would call the Police to remove us. There were a lot of problems with that because the Police would always come and make us move. When we would see the Police coming, we would begin to run automatically. We would have to grab our vegetables and fragile eggs and start running. This was an almost daily event. However, I continued to be steadfast and held onto my business.

Later, I met a woman who had a store on the street. She realized the problem that we were facing, with the Police. So she gave my wife and me a little entrance, which was between two places of business. It was an entrance with a table so that we could display our eggs and sell them from there. From that point on we started to win customers and my business started to grow.

The Electricity Commission

So every Friday, I would go back to the Chicken farm to get eggs to sell. One day the owner told me; *"Roland I am going to open a larger farm in Waller Field and I am going to have 140,000 chickens in that area. I am setting up some Pens there right now. Do you know anyone in the Electricity Commission, because I have received a letter from the Commission to have electricity? But this place is in the middle of that large base of vacant land where there is no current. This is* a lot of strenuous work for the carpenters to build these Pens by hand without electricity".

I understood that electricity was needed for the workers' saws, the grading machines for eggs, lights to grow the chickens and water pumps. So I told him I thought I could help him. The Lord, through someone my wife knew, caused me to be put in touch with the chief accountant in the Electricity Commission.

We told him the situation that my farmer friend was facing. The letter from the Commission stated that the farmer must give a capital contribution in the amount of about $11,000 to begin the project. There had to be poles, wires, and transformers which would involve a large work crew.

But the favor of the Lord was present! The letter was marked on the front with the words, *"Cancel"* and *"Please turn over"*. On the back it was marked with a fee of $300. So all my friend had to pay was $300 and once they received the receipt of payment; they would dispatch the crews! I took the letter to my farmer friend and of course, he was very happy! This was a tremendous blessing for him. The fee was paid; the receipt returned to the chief accountant, and the work began.

In appreciation for the money he had saved, my farmer friend gave us eggs without charging us and also gave us (4) goats. He mentioned that he had recently given away (11) milking cows. He said he would have given them to me, had we met earlier. I told him I was grateful for the goats and the cows were meant to bless someone else.

We continued to sell eggs from the small site in the city that we were given by the women business owner. She had a grandson, who was about 3-years-old at the time, and he would constantly cry. I asked her what his problem was. She said he saw other children with their animals at the park and he wanted a goat. The child had a hole in his heart, and the crying and sadness was not good for his health. She told me that she wanted to buy a goat for him.

I knew that God meant for me to be a blessing to her because she had been so kind to me, in giving me space to sell my eggs. So I brought the goats to her house and blessed her and her grandson. Not only did the child receive his desire for one goat, he had received (4) goats! Believe me, that entire household was very happy!

Remembering what Schambach said about giving; I was sowing a seed for my farm that I knew was on the way. I sowed it as an act of good faith and I believed the Lord would honor my faith.

Chapter Four

The Journey For My Farm

Do You Want Your Own Farm?

My farmer friend asked me one day, if I wanted to have my own farm and grow my own chickens. I told him *"Yes, I have always wanted to own a farm!"* He told me the old farmer near him, who had (5) acres, may be willing to sell to me. He said he would speak to him for me and then we could be neighbors.

When I went to see the old farmer's land, it was so striking, very beautiful. It had (2) Christmas Palm trees in the front of the house he lived in. In the back he had planted (150) Coconut trees. There were orchards at the sides of the farm, with citrus fruit, orange, grapefruit and lime; and at the very back end of the land there was a river. I was so happy the old farmer agreed to sell it! I fell in love with it and said: *"This is the place where I will grow my chickens"*.

Prior to that, I had been to a bank in Trinidad, called the Agricultural Development Bank. This Bank was set up in 1970 by the government to assist farmers in developing agriculture and farming. I had approached the Bank for a plucking machine for chickens, so that I could begin raising chickens at my home. I was informed that they did not make those kinds of loans; for plucking machines and chickens. They dealt with land; buying land for you and setting you up in business, only major loans. For example for fishermen, they would buy boats, nets, and whatever was needed for that type of business. The manager made it clear that they would only make big loans.

My farmer friend took me to that same Bank. I told him I had been there before. My friend took me to the manager and told him that I was his friend. He told him that the old farmer was interested in selling his farm and I wanted to buy it. He said; *"I must inform you that he has no money but he is going to go through this government program".*

Buying The Farm

The old man had agreed to sell, a loan officer was sent and the Bank agreed to purchase the land for me at $75,000. The Bank was actually just buying the rights to it, because there was a government lease for (99) years on the property. When the analysis was done and the loan was ready, I went to pick up the old gentleman to sign the papers. I expected him to be ready to go. When I arrived he said; *"Sit down Roland I need to tell you that I am not interested in selling the farm now".* I said; *"But the Bank finished the loan and everything is ready. I told you Friday that I was coming to get you to sign the papers!"* He said; *"I have changed my mind; I am not going to do it".*

At this point my wife was really, really upset; she refused to talk to him any further. You can probably imagine her disappointment and anger! He then said; *"I will do it, but I need $140,000".* And I said*; "The Bank is not going to give you that amount of money because they will say that you are speculating on the government's lands. I will have to go and inform the Bank".*

I went in and informed the manager about what happened with the old farmer changing his mind. He said there was no way they would give him $140,000. However, he told me that I could search for more land, and they would buy it for me and still set me up in farming.

Nevertheless, losing this first farm was still a huge disappointment for me. But I resolved to encourage myself in the Lord. After all, I had the word of the Lord, *"My farm is on the way and God will bring it to pass"*.

Chapter Five

Prayer For Double Portion

The "Double Portion" Prayer

On the way home I started to pray. I said; *"Lord; I know that You probably have something bigger for me"*. Later on that night I prayed alone. I liked to enjoy the beauty of the night sky, God's creation, when I prayed. I was staring at the moon, just enjoying the beauty of the moonlight. I said, *"Lord I know I have been turned down. I was so excited to receive the loan and it was prepared, but here the enemy has turned it down because this owner wants more money. However, Lord I pray that You will give me a double portion. Lord, this place was (5) acres of land, and I need a farm. I know

Brother Schambach has said, 'A farm is on the way'. Lord, You have got a bigger farm for me, so Lord I pray in the name of Jesus, Lord that You would give me a bigger farm; (10) acres of land with more Citrus trees, more Coconut trees and a river!"

My wife heard this prayer and jumped up and said; *"You are crazy! I have never heard anyone say a prayer like this before. If there is no place like this, you are telling God to make a place for you within the farming community".* But I continued to pray, rebuking her unbelief, and said; *"I believe God will do it!"*

The next morning I got up ready to look for land, but my wife refused to go with me based on the prayer I had prayed the night before. She told me it was impossible for God to give us what we had just lost, and on top of that, a double portion of (10) acres of land, with more Citrus trees, Coconut trees and a river! She said; *"The same thing we just lost and a double portion; that is just impossible!"*

But I said; *"I trust God!"* I left alone looking for land and returned home later without finding anything. My wife said; *"I know God's not going to do it!"* The second day I had the same result and mentioned to her; *"I did not receive a breakthrough today".* She replied; *"There is no way you can have a breakthrough; God's not going to do it!"*

On The Third Day

On the third day, God took my valley of trouble and turned it into a door of hope! I lived in the city of Diego Martin in the Village of Sierra Leone. As the third day was ending, I was led by the Holy Spirit to travel to Guanapo Arima. This area was known as *"The Congo"* and was also known for having a large number of wells. It's interesting that the Village of Sierra Leone where I lived and *"The Congo"* were both names that were associated with West Africa. I was led to Manuel Congo Road, a very lonely road, where I noticed there was some sugar cane. There was a small Village at the beginning as I entered. I drove about one mile down, on this stony road, past the sugar cane.

Then I saw some cows and a Chicken farm, and empty lands. I came upon a house with (2) Christmas Palm trees in front, and when I got out of the car, I saw Coconut trees at the back! So in my spirit I said; *"Lord this is exactly what I have been praying for! This is what You have revealed to me. You answered my prayer, this is the fulfillment!"*

So I took off my shoes and socks, stood on the property and placed my hand on the house; and I claimed that land! I said; *"Father I claim this land for my farm".* I got back into the car before someone saw me and thought I was crazy! But I decided to blow my horn to see if anyone would come out of the house. There seemed to be no one home.

As I was backing my car out of the driveway, this woman came out of the house and called to me. I returned and introduced myself to her. She told me that the man who lived on this land worked in the Battery factory in town. He did not own it; he was only the caretaker. She told me to come back the next day and he would be home. I was so excited; I went home and told my wife about the farm, at least the parts that I was able to see. Her unbelief was still evident when she said; *"Yes, but you're not sure if the owner will even sell it. You're not even sure it has Citrus trees and you're not sure if there is a river and even so you're not sure he will sell it to you".*

But I was not changed, I believed God! I went back on Friday to see the caretaker, his name was Duncan. I told him that I was interested in buying the property. He said that he would speak to the owner on Saturday and give me his answer on Monday. Before returning home, I decided to stop and get my eggs to sell on Saturday and Sunday. So I had my car filled with eggs. As I returned home, just a few hundred yards from home, the muffler fell off my car up to the exhaust! There was a lot of noise and smoke. I had to take the eggs out of the car into the house. I told my wife I would not be able to go the Market in the morning to sell these eggs. First I had to go the Welding Shop to have the muffler fixed. So I prayed that night; I knew the enemy was after me! But I resolved to be the first customer, early in the morning, to get my muffler fixed.

The Welding Shop – A Divine Connection

The next morning, while it was still dark, I went to the Welding Shop and was the very first customer. Then a man parked next to me. He walked over to me and said; *"Hello do you mind if I ask you a favor?"* I asked; *"What is the favor?"* He said; *"I know you were first but would you mind if I go in before you? We are Catholics, my children have to go to Choir and sing and I am a Rosarian; I look after the roses.*

And I have a lot of things to do today, so I would appreciate you allowing me to go first". I told him: *"Sure, no problem".* I have always believed that whatever I was praying and seeking God for; I should still do good deeds so I gave him the option to go in first!

So he parked his car in my spot and I took his spot. The Holy Spirit had it all planned this way! While waiting for the shop to open, (this Asian gentleman), walked over to my car, an old Austin Cambridge English car, and started a conversation. He noticed the number of egg carts in the back of my car and asked me if I sold eggs. *"Yes, I sell eggs";* I replied. I began to share my whole story with him about leaving my job, losing the first farm and the second one that I had just found on Thursday on Manuel Congo Road.

I told him that I had just fallen in love with the place and talked to the caretaker, about it on Friday. The caretaker promised to talk to the owner about selling to me on Saturday; and Monday, give me the owner's answer.

The man said; *"Explain to me again about the land you saw on Thursday and Friday".* I again described the details of the location. I told him what I saw in the front of the house and the trees I saw in back; and that the caretaker was to give me the owner's answer on Monday. He asked; *"Is the caretaker's name Duncan?"* I said, *"Yes"*. He then said; *"Oh, I am the owner of that land!"*

I was in shock and excited because I know what I prayed! I asked; *"Will you sell me the land?"* He said; *"Sure I will sell you the land"*. He immediately gave me his address and phone number and told me to come to his home on Monday. I told him I had to go to the Bank and let them know that I found this land and the owner is willing to sell to me.

I began to ask him details about the property. I asked; *"How many acres are there?"* He replied; *"(10) acres"*. I asked; *"I saw some Coconut trees in the back of that land; how many do you have?"* He replied; *"I remember when I bought the land it had a few trees but I planted (300) Coconut trees"*. I thought to myself; *"The first land had (150) Coconut trees and now this land has (300) plus and the first land was (5) acres and he had just told me his land is (10) acres!"* I then asked: *"What do you have at the side borders of the land?"* He said; *"I have Citrus trees; Orange, Portugal, Grapefruit and Lime!"* It was the same thing the first land had, but double!

Finally, I had to ask one more question. I asked; *"What else is there in the back of the land?* He replied; *"There is a river in the back of the land"*.

Chapter Six

Receiving The Double Portion

So I just laughed because I knew what I had prayed for! The Lord, in just a matter of days, had brought it to pass! It was truly the *"double portion"* blessing from the Lord! There was twice as much land and twice as many trees!

He said; *"I am going to sell you the land. Go to the Bank and make all of your necessary arrangements".* So I fixed my muffler and went home. I told my wife about it and she was excited and asked if he was really going to sell; and at what price. I told her that was the one thing I did not find out, but that I would go to Bank and tell them that I found the land and the owner is willing to sell. The Bank had told me they would go up to $250,000; I just had to let them know how much I needed. Now that there was progress, my wife now prayed with me and went with me on Monday to the Asian gentleman's home!

Meeting At The Owner's Home

When we arrived at the owner's home on Monday, there was a blue Rolls Royce parked in front of the gate. I knew the car belonged to one of the richest men on the island of Trinidad; a contractor! I knew for a fact that he owned (2) Rolls Royce automobiles. I told my wife who he was and we both wondered what he was doing there.

My wife began to say; *"Let's go, let's go! If this Millionaire is here, he is probably going to try to compete with you for the land and the Bank will not lend that much money!"* I said; *"No, the owner said that he would sell me the land"*. We walked to the entrance or gate. As this Millionaire was leaving the compound, he spoke aloud to the Asian gentleman; *"I will give you $250,000, and raise it up to half a million; just tell me how much you want for the land"*. At this point we knew he was talking about the same piece of land we wanted! My wife kept saying: *"Let's go, let's go! There is no way we can get that property for the price the Bank will pay!"* But I prayed; *"Lord, touch the heart of this Asian man so that he will accept the figure the Bank is willing to pay; the amount the Bank would say is reasonable for this property".* Also it was on my mind that this land was not government land but private property.

The Asian owners were still in the yard. They greeted us and the man said, *"Do you know who that man was?"* I said his name, admitting that I knew who he was. The owner then said; *"He came here to buy the land you want. You remember Duncan was supposed to come here on Saturday to see me. He did not come here but went to this man's place of business and told him you were interested in buying the place. Duncan wanted him to come and buy it, hoping to receive a bonus or commission from him. He just offered me $250,000 or more money, for the land you want! But I'm not going to sell to him. I gave you my word and you were quite honest to give me your space to have my muffler fixed first, so I will sell you the land!"*

Right at that precise moment, I could sense the Holy Spirit say to me; *"Ask him the price now before you go inside!"* I quickly asked the price of the land for me. He looked at me and my wife and then he looked at his wife, scratched his head, and said; *"Ok give me $70,000"*. As you can imagine, when he said $70,000, every part of the fabric of my being, every bone, tissue and cell of my body began to rejoice and praise God for that price! I told him; *"I will need something in writing for the Bank saying that you are willing to sell to me at that price"*. He told me to come into the house and gave me the deed, sketch of the land and a letter in writing; stating that he was selling the land to me for $70,000!

In the natural, this was impossible! Also unlike the other land, this was privately owned, not a government lease. My wife and I were stunned beyond belief and even she was now singing hymns and praising God for the miracle!

Chapter Seven

The First Obstacle

An Obstacle – 20% Capital Contribution

The next day I went to the Bank and told the manager about the land. I showed him the deed and the owner's letter of intent. He replied; *"You're crazy; that is impossible, how in the world did you find privately owned land, (10) acres for $70,000? I have been looking for land and have found nothing to compare to this and for this price!"*

So they sent a loan officer to visit and evaluate this new property first, before releasing the loan to purchase the land for my Chicken farm.

After the survey was done, I was told that there was a problem with the loan. I was told that because it was not government land like the first property, but private property, I needed a capital contribution of 20% or $14,000! After I paid the money then they would release the funds for everything I needed. He said he had forgotten to mention this to me! Again the doubting voices came through my wife. As you can imagine my wife was very angry that this bank manager did not seem to know his job and should have mentioned it before! But I continued to trust God!

But I thought; *"Oh my God, I am selling eggs, where am I going to get $14,000, I don't have $14 and where would I get $14,000?"* I felt led by the Lord to go and talk to my farmer friend, who I had only known for a matter of several weeks, actually a couple of months. I told him everything that had transpired concerning this new land I had found and I took him to see it. He agreed that it was good land for farming. But I said that I needed $14,000 and did not have the money and therefore could not follow through with the plan.

He said; *"No, I remember when I wanted electricity on my land, you helped me save thousands of dollars. You helped me, now my farm is in operation; and it is way advanced. So I know that you need the money; you have been buying eggs from me. So come with me".*

We went to see some of his larger customers and we collected $4,000 in cash. But we were still $10,000 short. Next he took me to his Bank and told them to make a check out to me for $10,000! I now had the $14,000! Again, I had only known him a matter of weeks, but because we helped him, he was returning the favor. My wife was there with me and could not believe that we had the money in just one day!

The following day, I went back to the bank manager with the $14,000. He said; *"Wait you came here; you are selling eggs, and you don't have $14. I tell you to raise the money and you come back the next day with $14,000. I just want to ask you something. I have been a bank manager all of these years, and I have never seen anything like this! I want to ask you something.* **Roland; Who is your God?** *Who is the God you serve? Are you involved in any form of witchcraft or the occult or a member of a Lodge?"* I said, *"No"*.

He went on to say; *"This is impossible! You lost the first land, now you have new land and I can't believe the price; and you had no money* *for the capital contribution for the land. Now you come back two days later with $14,000! Well now we can go ahead with the loan! Tell me **Roland; Who is your God?"*** This man was a Hindu and I was really able to be a witness to him about the grace and power of my God, the Lord Jesus Christ!

Chapter Eight

God's Hands Are Not Tied!

Another Obstacle – The License or Quota

I went back to check on the loan two days later. I talked to a different manager than the one I had previously seen. The first manager had been transferred to a different branch. I was told there was another problem! I was told that the Bank could not release the funds because I needed a License or Quota to grow chickens. I asked him to explain to me what License I needed. He told me that the government had to give me a License to grow chickens and without that, they could not release the loan. He expressed his apologies for not knowing this before. He gave me the name of the Poultry

Industry Council Committee (PICC), the place where I needed to get the License. When I informed my wife, she was angry at the Bank management again, for seemingly not knowing their jobs! She did not understand how they could not have known and informed us, that we needed a License to grow chickens! Again, she was upset and would not pray with me.

But I prayed and said to God: *"Lord You will not leave me halfway through; this farm will come to pass just like Brother Schambach said"*. So I went to the (PICC) to get the License. While there, I was told that the wait would be 2½ to 3 years! There were so many before me to be interviewed and it would probably be that long before I was contacted! I said to the Lord: *"Oh my God, this is impossible, I cannot wait this long!"* This problem, we now encountered, was by far the most challenging! In my mind, I just began rehearsing everything that happened to get me to that point.

I came back home and told my wife about this latest obstacle. I prayed: *"Lord, work a miracle, work a miracle; I cannot wait 2½ to 3 years. You have to do something and get me a Quota! Make a way in the wilderness for me Lord; make an opening for me!"* There was no way possible in the natural to get this paperwork because that was the only agency responsible for the License or Quota. No one else could give one to me and I would have to wait all of these years.

And of course my wife's faith was broken after these two events with the land. She said to me; *"God's hands are tied! God's hands are tied; there is no way in the natural, let us reason; you know logical reasoning! There is no way we can do this. You will have to give back the money to our farmer friend and give back the deed to the owner".* But I prayed; *"Lord in the Bible, I see NO WAY that Your hands are tied! You, Lord will work a way out!"*

I Must Inform The Owner

So now I had to decide who to visit first. The Lord revealed to my spirit to visit the owner and let him know. I asked my wife to go with me and she said; *"No way, God has failed us once, He just does not want to bless us! He is failing us a second time, I can't go through all of this! I give up! I give up! I will not go and tell this man a story like this!"* She would not praise, worship or pray at all.

While on the way to the owner's place, I kept hearing my wife's voice saying; *"God's hands are tied! God's hands are tied!"* The enemy was tormenting me also saying; *"There is no way possible to get the License; here are the facts. There are too many people ahead of you and there is no way you can do anything, you will lose the land because you cannot get the License".* I kept rebuking him, but he would begin over and over again; he just kept bugging me! Then I would hear my wife's voice again; *"God's hands are tied! God's hands are tied!"*

So I walked into the owner's home, telling him that I wanted to talk to him and his wife. I told them both about the problem and that I trusted God to work something out. When I told him and his wife; his wife was so sad and she prayed; *"Lord what can we do to assist Roland? We have come so far, he has reached so far; what can we do to help him?"* I said; *"I don't know; it all seems so impossible".* I could feel the enemy pressuring me again and I could hear my wife's voice; *"God's hands are tied! God's hands are tied!"*

However, all of a sudden, the owner said; *"Wait a minute; wait a minute!"* He remembered that when he purchased the land (10) years earlier, a friend had told him to go to the (PICC) and interview for this License or Quota. He had interviewed for that License and never used it!

He went straight to the drawer and found the License and handed it to me. His wife said; *"Oh my God Roland! God has answered your prayer, here is your Quota, now there is nothing to stop you from having your farm!"* The three of us began to rejoice and praise God!

Silencing The Voices!

When I walked out of his house with that Quota in my hand, I could no longer hear my wife's voice saying; *"God's hands are tied! God's hands are tied!"* That voice had finally left my ear! The oppressive forces of the enemy had left me also and I was free! As I walked to my car I felt as though I was on *"Cloud Nine"* as that expression goes. I felt as if I was walking in *"Space"*.

I got in my car and opened the other door and took the Quota, I kissed it and set it on the dashboard. I said; *"satan, I opened the door for you now, come and sit now and see the Quota that the Lord has given me! The Lord has given me a Quota, no way – no way could this have happened!"* The oppressive voices were now gone because I got the victory with the Quota!
When I told my wife what had transpired, she still had difficulty believing it at first. When she

realized that it was true, she began to rejoice. It was so powerful to realize that God looked into the future and had already made provision for me. He had made the way for me to have this land and grow chickens (10) years before! The Lord had this man get that Quota, even though he never used it; because He knew that I would someday occupy that land! Praise God!

Another thing I want to mention is that I offered to sign a promissory note or IOU to my farmer friend to pay him back for the $14,000. He did not want it, saying we were friends and he had given it to me! God was so good to show me such favor, that this man would give me that amount of money! Glory to God!

Chapter Nine

"Roland; Who Is Your God?"

Back To The Bank

When I went back to the Bank, with the Quota, the second manager, who was in fact a Muslim, was in shock. He just could not understand it!

He began to rehearse each event, *(Miracle of God),* that had happened to me beginning with the first property. He knew that it would have taken a long time to get a Quota, but there I was back the next day with one! He kept repeating that he did not understand it! The first manager, who was a Hindu, had asked; **"Roland; Who is your God?"** Now this second manager, who was a Muslim, began to ask the same question; ***"Roland; Who is your God? What God do you serve? Is this some form of witchcraft?"*** Again I could be a powerful witness for the Lord Jesus Christ and glorify His name! So now nothing would stand in the way of the loan.

Back To The (PICC)

I went back to the (PICC) with my Quota. The receptionist remembered me and said it was not my time and that I still had to wait for my interview. I told her that I had my Quota from the owner of the land, and showed it to her; asking her to transfer it to my name. She replied that it would require the members of the Board to meet and execute that transfer.

I was ushered into a room and questioned by the Board members. I was told that they would not accept the Quota or transfer it to my name. They asked me how much I had paid for it! Then they accused me of going to the owner's home and stealing it from him! They said that the owner had to come personally to the Board and confirm what I had said was true.

I explained the problem to the Asian owner and he was so kind and agreed to meet me at the

(PICC) the next morning. I was so excited that all of this was coming to an end, that I left my house without eating anything. The owner was there early and had brought me coffee and sandwiches! God is so good in His kindness toward me! The Asian owner appeared before the Board members and said that he was selling me his land. He also said, he had never used the Quota and had given it to me at no charge. So they agreed to transfer it. The original Quota was for 14,000 chickens and was upgraded to 20,000 when it was transferred to my name!

I went back to the Bank, and again the manager was in shock, but I finally received the loan for my farm! I established the farm and in my first year, as a new farmer, I was given the award of *"Small Farmer of the Year"* in 1981. Glory to God!

Again I remembered the words of Brother Schambach; *"We have prayed for you and the farm is on the way. God is going to bring it to pass"*. God brought it to life! I acquired the land and had my farm because the Lord had miraculously brought it to pass!

Exceeding Abundantly Above

This testimony about how the Lord brought this farm to me happened more than (30) years ago. I operated my farm for more than (10) years with great success and actually spent more than (21) years in agriculture. I will share just a few examples concerning the scale and magnitude of my farming experience.

Organic Farming

Even before I received my farm on Manuel Congo Road, I lived on an acre of land that was very fertile, near Cocoa Estates where they grew cocoa and sugar cane. I have always believed in organic farming and one year I planted *"pakchoi"*, a kind of long leaf spinach.

I sold some of my pakchoi to a man one Saturday and I was not aware there was an Agriculture Exhibition that day.

On Monday I happened to see the man again and he was with his 10-year-old son. The little boy said: *"Mr. Roland, we took your pakchoi to the Exhibition on Saturday and won a trophy!"* His father was very embarrassed as he quickly tried to quiet his son! I would have never known if the child had not blurted it out!

Chickens For KFC

At one point, I worked with Cannings Foods, Poultry Division; the company responsible for raising chickens for Kentucky Fried Chicken (KFC). As a farmer, I had to have the proper facilities including a large size Chicken Pen, and the proper electricity, watering system and feeders. I would receive 40,000 baby chicks, which I would raise for about (6) weeks before sending them to KFC. Vets from America and London would come and inspect my facilities, to ensure that there were high quality standards; and my farm always received the highest marks!

Mystery Abundance

In regard to my organic farming techniques, there has always seemed to be what I sometimes call *"mystery abundance"*. This, of course, is a mystery to the world; but not for those of us who know our God! His Word tells us; *"Now unto Him that is able to do exceeding abundantly above all that we ask or think, according to the power that worketh in us"* (Ephesians 3:20).

For instance there was the time, I planted pumpkins for this man who owned more than (50) acres of land. We shipped 21,000 pounds of pumpkins to Florida, in the U.S. In addition, on every Friday we sold 3,000 pounds to a couple of local supermarkets. One time I saw some people stealing (3) truckloads! I decided it was wisdom to let them take the pumpkins instead of risking my life!

Since coming to America, I recently convinced someone to let me grow tomatoes on empty space on their land. We found that there was also this same *"exceeding abundantly above"* or *"mystery abundance"* of tomatoes with very little effort! There was so much, family and friends could not eat them all! According to Joshua 1:8; if we remain focused on the Lord and His Word, we will be successful and prosperous!

Reflections

I believe at this point it is important for me to share this fact. My wife, at that time, is now my former wife. During the mid 1980's, she decided that she wanted to go in a different direction and initiated proceedings to dissolve our marriage. I had no choice in the matter. As painful as that was, I had to respect her decision and I blessed her then, and I bless her now. I am now remarried to a wonderful woman who is able to share in the calling the Lord has placed on my life. Praise God for blessing and restoration!

Brothers and Sisters when I reflect back on what the Lord did for me in Trinidad, I think of Joseph. I read the scriptures in Genesis about Joseph and what God did in his life; by sending him ahead to Egypt to make provision for His people. I now realize that the Lord, in Trinidad, was preparing me to do the same thing again. The Lord's words were; *"What I did for you in Trinidad, I will bless you and give you a double portion blessing again here in America. So take this message to the Churches and give this testimony!"*

The word of the Lord came again to me in confirmation. He said; *"I'm going to use you as a 'Moses' to lead the children out of hardship and bring them to the land of milk and honey"*. So, now I fully realize that this is what the Lord has called me to do. I promised Him that I would be obedient, steadfast, study, meditate, read the Word and never turn to the left or the right.

Right now I want to share with you, my Brothers and Sisters, that there is going to come a time in your life when you will face problems like I faced. There will come a time when you will reach and face your own *"Red Sea"*. There will be obstacles facing you, (4) of them! The Red Sea in the Front and the enemy army will be at your back and the mountains on each side; left and right, east and west. You have to go on and the army is coming after. The only thing for the children of God to do is look up to Him, *"Who is the Author and Finisher"* of your faith. This is what I did; this is how I trusted the Lord and He has brought these things to pass in my life!

Why Farming?

Some of you may ask; *"Why is the Lord emphasizing farming?"* Let's take a look at these familiar scriptures in the book of Luke.

Luke 4:18-19
The Spirit of the Lord is upon me, because he hath anointed me to preach the gospel to the poor; he hath sent me to heal the

brokenhearted, to preach deliverance to the captives, and recovering of sight to the blind, to set at liberty them that are bruised, To preach the acceptable year of the Lord.

I believe the reason why the Church of Jesus Christ and the world are not experiencing God's fullest blessing; is because we have not fulfilled the first part of Luke 4:18! We have not preached the gospel or *"good news"* to the poor! The good news for them is that they don't have to be poor or hungry anymore!

We have not received the Lord's heart and compassion for the poor and there is so much poverty and hunger in the world! God is holding us, His Church, accountable for not doing our part. Jesus said in Matthew 26:11; *"For ye have the poor always with you; but me ye have not always"*. That was not to say we should ignore them, but Jesus was letting us know that we are to take care of the poor after His death.

Just as Joseph was sent ahead to Egypt to prepare provision for the famine, I believe this is our mandate also. Think of how God's favor and wisdom were upon Joseph to accomplish the task of feeding and preserving not only his family, but the world (Genesis 45:7-8)! Famine is coming and a massive food shortage. The poor and needy in the U.S. and around the world have already existed in hunger. Now, with the recent economic downturn and natural disasters; those figures are multiplied and growing. Think of all the empty and unused land that could be used to farm and grow food! Imagine how awesome it would be if each Church would begin a *"Farm Project"* and grow food in their area to feed those in need!

In Isaiah 58:6-12, the Lord is talking about the results of His chosen fast. These results sound very much like Luke 4:18. He is talking about breaking the chains of injustice and oppression over His people, and taking care of the poor, hungry and needy. The Lord declares that if we will do this, then we will experience healing, deliverance, restoration and the Glory of God!

Psalms 41:1-2
Blessed is he that considereth the poor: the LORD will deliver him in time of trouble. The LORD will preserve him, and keep him alive; and he shall be blessed upon the earth: and thou wilt not deliver him unto the will of his enemies.

I believe my mandate is to *"Wake Up"* the Body of Christ to these possibilities. We see the heart of Jesus when He had compassion on the multitudes following Him for (3) days (Matthew 15:32:39). Jesus said in effect; *"I just can't send them away fasting and hungry or they will faint along the way"*. So He supernaturally fed them because He had so much compassion and was looking at their condition at that moment.

So it's not just feeding the poor, it is being moved with the compassion of the Father's heart to do so. We are talking about eventually feeding multitudes of people! Think of how many people will be drawn to Christ as we meet this basic physical need!

The Lord makes us a wonderful promise in Psalm 41. If we consider the poor, the Lord will preserve us and deliver us out of trouble; and bless us beyond measure!

That is why I have written this book and given my testimony. The Lord has highly favored me and used me in farming in Trinidad; and He has promised to bring a *"double portion blessing"* to America! All praise and glory to our wise and compassionate God!

Chapter Ten

Bringing Life Into The Village
(Road, Water, Electricity)

Fixing The Road

When I first started my farm, there were a lot of problems with the road due to excavations. On each side of the road there was gravel and it was destroying the foundation of the road. Workers were digging too deep and too close to the road, much more than the government specification had allowed, so the road was shifting. There were farmers and residents in the area who had tried to get the government to fix the road, but were unsuccessful. It really was a very stony and bumpy road! I began to pray about it and ask God for His help. I was able to get some of the residents to sign a petition to have the road resurfaced, and I took it to the government authorities. Many people in the Village thought we were crazy, saying; *"This could never happen!"*

But, to their amazement, the authorities came and surveyed the road and took pictures! As a matter of fact, it was in the newspapers and on television and very soon after, the road was fixed, graded and leveled off! Praise God!

Getting Pipe-Born Water

The second thing we needed for my farm was water. In that area where I started the farm, we had no running water. Most people used water from wells and used a manual hand pump to get water for their animals. But I knew that kind of work was too strenuous for the 20,000 to 40,000 chickens I planned to have! So I decided to go to the authorities in charge of Water and Sewage in Trinidad. There were farms further up the road than I and these farmers just thought I was crazy. They felt we had only been able to get the road fixed because enough people lived there. But they believed that it would not be at all profitable for the authorities to put water lines where we were located. Again, I got the farmers and people around to sign a petition and took it to the Water and Sewage Authority (WASA). I spoke to the head engineer and he came with officers. They measured the distance from where the line ended to my farm and it was about one mile.

This was in December and the engineer told me that they had closed off all financing for the year. The head engineer said there was nothing he could do, but maybe they could get water for us the next year. But he said he would continue to work on it.

The next thing I knew, during the week between Christmas and New Year's Day, I saw a truck coming up the road and the driver asked for *"Roland"*. And I said; *"I am Roland"*. The truck was filled with, (4) inch diameter (20) foot long, PVC pipes for the water main! The trucker said the head engineer authorized him to bring the pipe and leave it on my property. So I signed for it, as the one responsible for the pipe.

Later that same afternoon I saw a tractor coming up the road and the operator asked for *"Roland"*. I said; *"I am Roland"*. He said; *"You are a lucky man! I have worked for WASA for a number of years, and my father before me, and I took over the contract. This is a brand new tractor; I just left the store with it and received a call from the head engineer. He said, 'I want you to go to Manuel Congo Road and find that farmer named Roland. You can leave your tractor with him, it will be safe there'".*

Within a couple of days the one mile distance had been dug and the pipe laid down! Before the end of that year we had pipe-born water for my farm! This was not just my blessing; but my farmer neighbors now had water for their chickens, cows and even their crops. All praise and glory to God! So far the Lord had blessed this community with having the road fixed and now we all had pipe-born water!

"Lord We Need Electricity!"

The next thing I needed was electricity. When I moved into the area, there were no lights, no poles, transformers, or anything! So I went to the authorities in charge of electricity. I spoke to the chief construction engineer and then eventually the engineer assigned to that area.

They came and did a survey and within a short time they sent crews and set up everything we needed. It was also a major blessing that there was no capital contribution required from the farmers! Now we were all able to have electricity in our homes and for our farms!

Reflections

Through the Lord's divine favor and blessings, we were able to get these (3) things corrected! After that I remember a man named Leslie, who lived in the Village, came to me. He said; *"Roland you came to this Village and it's like you opened a book and showed the people in this Village, and in this area, how to do business and how to prosper. Since you have come here, you have brought lights, water, and had the road fixed. So you have been a blessing to this area! You have brought life into this Village!"*

As I reflect upon what Leslie said to me; I am reminded of Isaiah 62:10. It says; we are to go through the gates, remove the stones and smooth out the highway for the people; raising a banner for the entire world to see!

I gave all honor and glory to God for blessing me and causing me to be a blessing to others! We serve an awesome God! Sometimes, we fail to understand just how powerful He is! When we truly understand the depth of His love, mercy and compassion for us; we are in a position to receive God's best. Then our lives will be blessed to be a blessing!

Chapter Eleven

The Crippled Man

I now had my farm running with great success. As mentioned before, I was named *"Small Farmer of the Year"* in 1981. I had a neighbor not far from my farm, who had (6) acres of land. He was crippled and would come to my farm and get coconuts, citrus fruit and eggs to sell at the Market. Although, the previous caretaker charged him for the fruit and produce, I felt led by the Lord to *"give"* it to him and everything else he needed. He would come on Friday with his son; go to the Market on Friday and all day Saturday and return home Sunday afternoon.

He would stay in a small shack all of that time. I began to take him to the Market myself and pick him up on Sundays. We became close friends and I called him *"Dad"*.

"Lord, What Can I Do To Help Dad?"

I began to think of him being crippled, and in his condition, trying to take care of his family. I began to pray about him, asking God what else I could do for him.

I went to his home one day and said; *"Dad I want to ask you a question if you don't mind"*. He replied; *"What is it Roland?"* After I confirmed that he had (6) acres of land, I continued. I said; *"You have enough land to grow 20,000 chickens; would you like to be a farmer?"* He started to laugh and said; *"Roland, what are you telling me? I have no money: I have no experience, and I don't know anything about chickens. How can I do this? You are the one who knows about chickens and farming!"* I said; *"I will pray and I will assist you and God will make this possible!"*

So my first step was to go to the Bank and ask for a loan. The second step was to go to the company I was contracted to and find out if they would give him a contract also. I got positive responses from both places. He was shocked and amazed that I was doing this for him! Due to his age, the only thing the Bank required was that his property be transferred into his daughter's name; and she was able to secure the loan!

From Poverty To Abundance!

My work on *"Dad's"* behalf was my gift to him. So I handled the loan money for him. I rented the tractor to grade the land in order to make the Chicken Pen sites and I drew the sketches. I also estimated the material needed and purchased everything for the building of the Pens. *"Dad"* got help from neighbors, friends and family to build the Pens. Praise God; we never had to pay for that part!

I knew all of the subcontractors who would give us the best price. I had the electrician who wired my house and farm to wire the Pens for him. I built the watering system for the chickens, because I had already done this system for my farm.

I saved so much money there was a sizeable amount of the loan left! *"Dad"* was able to purchase a vehicle for the farm. He also had enough cash to operate the farm until it began to show a profit, without being stressed by any unforeseen event! The Inspectors came and said everything was up to standard for growing chickens!

Reflections

That same year *"Dad"* began his farm, he was named *"Small Farmer of the Year"*. It was such an outstanding farm and he went from a life of poverty to a life of abundance! Praise God for his loving kindness and tender mercies!

One day I asked *"Dad"* how he became crippled. I found out that he had been working for a radio station in Trinidad when he had a stroke that left him crippled. He had to give up his job and it reduced to him to poverty and having to sell produce at the Market to provide for his family.

The compassion and love that God had for this man, was placed in my spirit. I remember first noticing him one day soon after I started my farm. He was taking water from a well in the back of his land. So I paid his fee to WASA for him to have pipe-born water on his land.

God used me to bring blessing to this man's life. What a wonderful, glorious way to live – to bring the abundance of heaven to the people God loves!

Chapter Twelve

The Donkey Named "Roland"

I Need A Donkey

As I began to operate my farm, I decided I needed a donkey because I had a large amount of land and could find many uses for one. In Trinidad, donkeys were mainly used to pull carts. People would load their carts with coconuts and take them to the cities, parks and different places to be sold.

One of my workers knew a man wanting to sell his donkey, because he had purchased a truck to sell his coconuts. Since he no longer had a need for the donkey, my worker thought we should go and see this man.

In Trinidad, the normal price for a donkey would be between $300 and $400. So one day my worker and I went to see this donkey. When we arrived the owner was not there but his wife was. The first thing I noticed was that the donkey was tied to a bamboo patch of trees with a rope about (15) feet long. Right along the bamboo patch the donkey had eaten everything in sight within his reach! There was nothing left to eat and there was an empty bucket, with no water! The man had left the donkey out there in the hot sun with no water and nothing to eat. The donkey was nothing but skin and bones, very emaciated! The man's wife even commented that the donkey would probably be dead shortly.

Not long after, the man came and I asked him; *"Well how much are you going to charge me for this donkey?"* He replied; *"This donkey; look just give me $50".* I repeated the price he quoted; *"$50 for the donkey".* In Trinidad we have very large, huge high bred goats. This donkey looked like a big ram goat because he was so small you could see his bones and ribs! So we decided to take the donkey. My worker and I alone, were able to lift the donkey onto the truck because he was so light! This poor donkey was so light and so weak; he could hardly stand and was just falling down. But it was very easy for us to lift him onto the truck to take him back to my farm.

Bringing The Donkey Home

This was on a Saturday and as we left, we had to pass through a very busy high traffic area. It was midday and there was a Mall and a lot of traffic. As we were driving through the Mall area and the city, people in their cars were saying; *"Oh my God you are taking advantage of that donkey! Look at that donkey! Look at how skinny that donkey is!"* My truck had an open tray in the back, so they could clearly see the condition of the donkey. They could also see that he could not even stand up in the truck! I remember that the little children, in particular, were pointing and laughing at the donkey and us. People were saying; *"What are you all doing to that donkey?"*

We were happy to finally get to my farm! My worker and I lifted the donkey out of the truck the same way we had placed him in there, by placing our hands under his tummy.

On the farm, I had all the different types of medication for the chickens. I had molasses and plenty of grass since I had (10) acres of land. So I built a place to put the donkey. I tied him and he began to eat the grass. I had the Vet, when he came to visit the chickens and other animals, take a look at him. He said, *"Yes you can give him vitamins and give him plenty of water and put the molasses in his water to boost his appetite"*.

It was amazing how quick that donkey got his size and strength back and started to run around! He was just so strong; he was a *"Jack"* (the name for a male donkey). He had started to jump and to kick, so I decided it was time to ride him. On the farm I had these old feed bags. So I tied (4) or (5) of them together to make a saddle and tied them on his back. All of my workers were afraid to ride him because he would jump and kick. I declared to them without fear; *"I will ride him!"*

The Wildest Ride Of My Life!

I remember the very first day I rode that donkey was on Palm Sunday! So I climbed on this donkey and by the way he was so smart! I remember there was a big drain, about (5) to (6) feet wide with water, it was pretty deep. This donkey just took off! I could not control him, he started to run and he jumped that drain! I thought I would be able to jump off but he jumped that drain, that huge drain, with me on him! At that point it occurred to me, *(a little too late),* that he had probably never been ridden because he was trying to throw me off!

Then he started running through a barrier with trees and where there were low-lying branches, he would run under those branches. He was trying so hard to knock me off that I had to lie down on him with my head close to his head to keep from falling off!

A Donkey In The Kitchen!

The donkey continued to the next farm. The farms were pretty far apart and this was the farm next to me. This farmer had a sister who was living on the farm in the farmhouse. The kitchen had an extension with pillars and a section with a big entrance. And I still could not control this donkey! The woman was sitting on the step to the kitchen combing her daughter's hair. The donkey went straight through the kitchen in one door and out the other! The woman shouted; *"What is this?!"*

Her daughter said; *"Mommy, its Roland on a donkey's back!"*

Later that afternoon, when I finally managed to get back home *(in one piece),* my neighbor came and asked me what happened. He heard the report about me, on a donkey, going through his kitchen! I think he was really having trouble believing it! He asked; *"Do you have a donkey?"* Even though he was next to me, our farms were far apart due to the acreage. He would usually come by on weekends and he did not know I had a donkey. So he saw the donkey and asked; *"Oh is that the animal?"* I said; *"Yes, sorry, but I just couldn't control him!"*

Look, It's Roland Riding A Donkey!

After going through my neighbor's kitchen, the donkey continued and went back onto the road and kept going down through the Village! The people came out of their houses and watched me. The children were saying; *"Look, Roland is riding a donkey, Brother Roland is riding a donkey!"* Since it was Palm Sunday, Easter time, you can imagine what an incredible picture that was! So I was really identified with that donkey from that time on!

During that week, I continued to ride him and eventually my workers gained the courage to ride him too!

Another Strange Event

Another strange event happened with that donkey. That same week on Good Friday, the donkey ran away from the farm and ran down the street. When some of the neighbors' children saw him, they knew he belonged to me. He was tame with them, so they held him and took him to one of their farms. Then they got paint and on the whole side of the donkey, they marked *"Roland"*. They *"marked"* the donkey with my name! Then they let him go and since he knew his home, he started running back to the farm. It became quite a joke among the children saying: *"Look, Roland is running up the street!"* They were laughing and making fun of me and the donkey! The next thing we knew we saw the donkey running back to my farm, with *"Roland"* marked on his side! My workers and I had great fun and laughter because of these (2) events between Palm Sunday and that day, Good Friday! So we took the donkey and washed the paint off of him.

His Last Days

Animals would normally go to the trees and scratch their skin. We had a lot of bamboo trees with sharp edges and I did not know my donkey scratched his inner ear on those trees and got an ear infection. I was feeding him and taking care of him and I noticed he was getting smaller. The Vet found the problem, sprayed the ear, and he was well again and regained his size and strength. We used him quite a bit on the farm for pulling the cart with the chicken manure from the Pens. We also used him to cut the grass and that sort of thing, he was very useful.

Later, the donkey got another ear infection, most likely the same way as before. He had begun to act crazy because it had penetrated into his brain. The Vet said that this infection was worse than the first time and he would not live. So eventually the donkey died and even his burial was very strange. We dug a hole to bury the donkey and evidently it was not deep enough. The donkey was placed on his back and the legs were bent down and he was covered. But his four legs kept popping out and it happened several times! I thought; *"Oh my God, what is happening here?"* Eventually we did get him pinned down and buried!

Reflections

When I reflect upon this donkey, there were so many strange events connected with him; from the time we brought him home when he was just skin and bones, and emaciated. There was his quick healing and recovery from the brink of death, which was somewhat miraculous. There was my first very *"wild"* ride through the Village on Palm Sunday! Also there was his Good Friday *"marking"* and identification with my name, *"Roland"*, painted on him. Last of all, there was this very strange burial!

Called To Be A Prophet

One night recently, I was with my dear friends, Prophets Lois Brinkley and Chiz Chickwendu. I recall saying; *"I don't know why I'm telling you this, but I feel led by the Lord to share this story with you"*. I began to tell them all about the strange events concerning this donkey. After all of these years, the Lord used Prophet Chiz to give me clarity on those events surrounding the donkey.

This is what the Spirit of the Lord said through him. *"God has clearly marked you as a prophet. It is as if he wrote on a tablet for you to see, in no uncertain terms that you are called to be a prophet! You are called BY NAME, as Cyrus was called by name. This designation was made clear the moment those children wrote your name on the donkey. God made it clear to you and to all who have eyes to see and read that you are a prophet."*

My friend went on to explain to me that: *"Animals in the scriptures are identified with certain assignments and callings. They are for us, symbols that indicate the nature of our task and work in the Kingdom of God. There are two animals of great significance, the ox and the donkey. The ox is symbolic of the Apostle whose work is to break fallow ground with the yoke placed on him.*

The Apostle of our confession would say; 'Come unto me all ye that labor and are heavy laden, and I will give you rest. Take my yoke upon you and learn of me' (Matthew 11:28-29). The strength of the ox is harnessed to grind out the meal. Paul tied the symbolism of the ox to the apostolic task, saying; 'do not muzzle the ox which grinds out the grain' (1 Timothy 5:18). The donkey is symbolic of the prophet and his assignment. He bears the burden of the Lord and perseveres with the load until the work is complete".

For me this was a powerful moment! God again brought confirmation to me concerning my purpose and destiny. I was called to bear the burden or heart of the Lord! I want to be used to reflect His love and compassion in all that I do. If only we could grasp how loving and compassionate the Lord is toward us!

Again I remembered the words of the Lord to me. *"What I did for you in Trinidad, I will bless you and give you a double portion blessing again here in America. So take this message to the Churches and give this testimony!"* The Lord gave me further confirmation when He said; *"I'm going to use you as a 'Moses' to lead the children out of hardship and bring them to the land of milk and honey".* Thank You Lord for counting me worthy to bear Your heart!

Final Note

My friend, Prophet Chiz, went on to write a fascinating complete profile on the *"Donkey"*. If you would like to know more about this, I have included the *"Donkey's Prophetic Signature"* in Appendix A.

Final Reflections

Editor

I have been honored to know and enjoy fellowship with Brother Roland. As Editor of this first volume, I have been thoroughly blessed by these awesome testimonies of the love, grace and power of our Lord! There are many more testimonies of what our God has done in his life and the lives of others he has come in contact with. We will bring them forth in the next volumes.

The testimonies throughout this book reveal that Brother Roland Sadoo is indeed a unique Prophet. As mentioned earlier, his life is an illustration of the type of ministry that Elijah walked in. The Lord has said about him; *"Roland is being used as an artist's paint brush in My hands, brushing strokes to create these portraits and masterpieces"*. Ephesians 2:10 confirms; *"For we are God's masterpiece. He has created us anew in Christ Jesus, so we can do the good things he planned for us long ago"*.

James 5:17-18
Elias was a man subject to like passions as we are and he prayed earnestly that it might not rain: and it rained not on the earth by the space of three years and six months. And he prayed again, and the heaven gave rain, and the earth brought forth her fruit.

I think it is significant that there is this New Testament reference about Elijah. This reference appears where James is revealing the power in *"the prayer of faith"* or *"effectual fervent prayer!"* The life of Elijah shows us that he was no ordinary Prophet; he was a prototype or model of a New Testament king-priest!

Brother Roland is walking in dominion and authority, declaring the Word of God. He also has communion and fellowship with the Lord and intercedes on behalf of others. That is the essence of our ministry as king-priests unto God!

The Lord Jesus Christ came to earth as our great example of an *"Apostle and High Priest (King-Priest)"*. In His great eternal ministry, He is seated on the right hand of the Father, ever living to make intercession for us! Hebrews 3:1 states; *"Wherefore, holy brethren, partakers of the heavenly calling, consider the Apostle and High Priest of our profession, Christ Jesus".* It is our heavenly or holy calling to follow the example of our Lord Jesus Christ as a *"royal priesthood"* (kings and priests).

The Lord Jesus Christ purchased this king-priest ministry for us on the Cross of Calvary when He shed His precious Blood! This truth is found in the following scriptures.

1 Peter 2:9
But ye are a chosen generation, a ROYAL PRIESTHOOD, an holy nation, a peculiar people; that ye should shew forth the praises of him who hath called you out of darkness into his marvellous light:

Revelation 1:5-6
....Unto him that loved us, and washed us from our sins in his own blood, And hath made us KINGS AND PRIESTS unto God and his Father; to him be glory and dominion for ever and ever. Amen.

Revelation 5:9-10
....For thou wast slain, and hast redeemed us to God by thy blood out of every kindred, and tongue, and people, and nation; And hast made us unto our God KINGS AND PRIESTS: and we shall reign on the earth.

We need to understand that this ministry is the highest in the earth! This is what the Blood of Jesus MADE us! How can we get any higher than that? He made us ALL to walk in victory, prosperity, power, and dominion! This is our destiny and we are called to the kingdom for a time such as this! Let's begin to embrace who we are! The Word tells us that John the Baptist came in the power and anointing of Elijah to prepare the way for the Lord Jesus Christ. We were created to walk in this *"Elijah Anointing"*, king-priests, to prepare the way for the Second Coming of the Lord!

Brother Roland has made a decision not to just sit on the sidelines of life, and allow situations and circumstances dictate his destiny. He has pressed through and shown us how one man, in pursuit of his purpose and destiny could bless so many others. He changed the atmosphere for so many because he was willing to pray, worship, intercede and pursue the presence of God! We should be encouraged to do the same! God has placed gifts inside of each one of us that will bless this world and bring glory to Him!

I think it's important right now to bring to your remembrance what the Lord revealed to Brother

Roland about his calling and destiny. This is what was recorded in the first chapter.

"My son what you did not know was that in Trinidad, beginning thirty years ago, I was preparing you for what I Am going to do with you, in this country, in America. I want you to go to the Churches and share this testimony and let the Believers know I Am the God of all flesh and nothing is too hard for Me! What I have done for you in Trinidad, I Am going to do for them. This testimony is NOT for the outsiders to the Church or the unbelievers. They can listen to it and partake of some of the blessings. Through which, they will begin to learn how to trust Me and then they will be drawn to Me. But this testimony is for the Believers, the Body of Christ, so that they will know how to trust Me to the fullest!"

Saints, if we have a covenant relationship with God, and passionately pursue His presence, He will begin to do these things for us! Brother Roland's testimony is meant to encourage us to trust God and walk in our destiny and purpose!

If you have a hunger to know the Lord, hear His voice and find your purpose and destiny; make this your prayer based on Ephesians 1:17-18.

Dear Heavenly Father,

I come to You in the name of the Lord Jesus Christ. Father, I pray that You would grant me the Spirit of Wisdom and Revelation in the knowledge of You. I pray for my 'heart eyes' to be flooded with light so that I may know the hope of Your calling and my glorious inheritance in You.

If you have never received Jesus Christ as your Lord and Savior and want to be in covenant with Him; please say this prayer out loud.

Dear Heavenly Father,

I come to You in the name of the Lord Jesus Christ. I repent of my sins and I ask for Your forgiveness. I now confess that Jesus is my Lord and Savior and I believe in my heart that He died for me and was raised from the dead. I ask You Jesus to come into my heart and live Your life through me. At this moment I believe that I am born again by an act of Your love, grace and mercy. Thank You for saving my soul. Amen.

Romans 10:9-10
That if thou shalt confess with thy mouth the Lord Jesus, and shalt believe in thine heart that God hath raised him from the dead, thou shalt be saved. For with the heart man believeth unto righteousness; and with the mouth confession is made unto salvation.

The End-Time Glory

Now we are ALL destined and ready to walk in the Glory of God in these end times! We are, in fact, positioned and ready for the *"Rain of God's Blessings"*. The earth is getting darker, but we are the *"Children of Light"*, the Lord's mighty army of king-priests! We are to arise and shine for the Glory of the Lord shall be seen upon us!

Isaiah 60:1

Arise, shine; for thy light is come, and the Glory of the LORD is risen upon thee.

Appendix A

Donkey's Prophetic Signature

By Chiz C. Chikwendu

I was in a place where God was showing me a lot of things through dreams and scriptures, and I really sought to understand the things I was seeing. It took me a while to realize that sometimes God wants to share things without necessarily wanting you to do anything about it. We are His friends and He tells His secrets to His friends. Sometimes we try to *"intervene via intercession to save the day"*, thinking that is what He wants. Sometimes He just wants someone to take His yoke and bear the burden. We, in the prophetic, are so familiar with visions. We celebrate the eagle as a symbol of the prophetic because of the keen vision and insight associated with it.

However, we do not always remember that there is a weight associated with the revelation. This is why the prophets would say, *"the burden of the Lord..."*

In my walk I have found that the things I knew caused me sometimes to be miserable, because we (the Body of Christ) are so far removed from where we could be. We seem to be our own enemies. I would have to agree with the sentiments of King Solomon in Ecclesiastes 7:4, where he says that *"the heart of the wise is in the house of mourning"*. Sometimes you wish you didn't know what you knew. It was from this realization that I began to pay more attention to the donkey as a burden-bearer in the scriptures, not knowing that there would be a burst of insight. It encouraged me to know that a prophet can soar like an eagle to see from an elevated place, the lay of the land, but would have to bend his back like a donkey to labor to enter into that rest.

The remainder of this writing will focus on the donkey's prophetic signature as it appears to us in the scriptures.

Donkey And Burden Bearing

The first instance that the donkey is associated with the prophetic is in the book of Genesis 49, when Jacob blessed his sons. He blessed Issachar with his own blessing as follows:

Genesis 49:14-15
"Issachar is a strong donkey, Lying down between two burdens; He saw that rest was good, And that the land was pleasant; He bowed his shoulder to bear a burden, And became a band of slaves".

The donkey is usually saddled with two burdens, one on either side of its back. It is a beast of burden, which is significant of the work of the prophet – that is, to bear the burden of the Lord. In the scriptures, prophets would say, *"the burden of the Lord is upon me"*.

Jacob prophesied that Issachar would be willing to bear the burden of work, and was willing to *"labor to enter into the rest"* which is in the land. Scriptures would go on to illustrate the prophetic dimension of the tribe of Issachar in 1 Chronicles 12:32-33.

"And of the children of Issachar which were men who had understanding of the times, to know what Israel ought to do, the heads of them were two hundred; and all their brethren were at their command".

Understanding the times and providing counsel on what ought to be done is the work of the prophetic. This is what catapulted Joseph from the prison to the palace. So the prophet labors, as with the donkey, to bear this burden of insight and understanding.

Donkey And The Prophetic Utterance

The prophetic signature of the donkey appears again in the book of Numbers, Chapter 22. King Balaak of Moab tries to recruit the prophet Balaam to curse Israel. As the story goes, God initially warns Balaam not to go with the messengers of Balaak. However, due to the pressure and allure of the reward of divination, Balaam consents to go with the messengers of Balaak; thinking that God had granted him permission to go.

As he was on his way to meet Balaak, an angel of the Lord stood in the way to confront Balaam because God considered his (Balaam's) way (undertaking) perverse before Him. The donkey which Balaam had been riding ever since the day he (Balaam) got the donkey, refused to move for fear of the angel. Balaam beat the donkey cruelly until God loosed the tongue of the donkey to speak intelligible words. The donkey confronted the prophet regarding his (the donkey's) faithfulness to the prophet. At which time God opened the eyes of the prophet to see the angel that had been standing in the way, ready to kill the prophet and let the donkey go free.

The scriptures, through the Apostle Peter, would later describe this event, as a time when *"the donkey, (through his speech), restrained the madness of the prophet"* (2 Peter 2:16). Balaam learned a critical lesson from the acts and words of the donkey that day, namely: *"God is not a man that He should lie, nor the son of man that He should change His mind"*. If God's original intention was for Balaam not to go meet Balaak to curse Israel, then God was not going to change His mind about that same intention.

The Prophet Sent To Bethel

This was a lesson that another prophet failed to learn, and again, God had to bring the donkey to bear witness to this same truth. In the book of 1 Kings 13, we are introduced to a prophet from Judah, sent to Bethel, to deliver a word. God clearly commanded the prophet what words to speak, and charged him not to eat or drink in Bethel and to return to Judah through another route.

After delivering the word given to him by God, this prophet allowed himself to be convinced by another prophet that God had changed His mind; about the command to not eat or drink in that territory. Subsequently the prophet, after having disobeyed the command given to him, went on his way and was assailed by a lion which killed him and did not eat him.

The supernatural nature of this event is evident in the fact that a donkey was present staring at the body of this prophet along with the wild lion which killed the prophet. The lion did not eat the corpse nor tear the donkey.

1 Kings 13:28
Then he went and found his corpse thrown on the road, and the donkey and the lion standing by the corpse. The lion had not eaten the corpse nor torn the donkey.

So the donkey bore testimony to this prophet, as it did to Balaam, that God does not lie or change His mind. Also a prophet that is *"stiff-necked"* is to be killed.

Donkey And The Stiff-Necked Prophet

The scriptures will again point to the donkey as representation of the prophetic voice of God by the manner of punishment which is meted out to the disobedient prophet. If you think God's judgment of the prophet from Judah was harsh, then examine the fate of the prophet whose sins cannot be atoned for or redeemed.

Exodus 34:19-20
"All that open the womb are Mine, and every male firstborn among your livestock, whether ox or sheep. <u>But the firstborn of a donkey you shall redeem with a lamb. And if you will not redeem him, then you shall break his neck</u>".

In the book of Exodus, as referenced above, God made it clear to Moses and Israel that each firstborn of the donkey must be redeemed; (He only placed this requirement on the first born of man and donkey). The firstborn of the donkey who is not redeemed, its neck shall be broken.

The prophetic symbolism of the *"unredeemed donkey"* and the *"stiff-necked prophet"* is illustrated in the life of Eli. Eli was the priest of God in Shiloh, but he was also the prophetic voice to Israel; as he stood in the place of the high priest as an intercessor between Israel and God. Consequently when Eli's sons became devilish (sons of Belial) in their behavior, and were not rebuked by their father, Eli too became disobedient and honored his sons above God. He became stiff-necked about the issue to the point that God declared that the sins of Eli's house would not be atoned for. There would be no redemption.

1 Samuel 13:11-14
And the LORD said to Samuel, Behold, I will do a thing in Israel, at which both the ears of every one that heareth it shall tingle. In that day I will perform against Eli all things which I have spoken concerning his house: when I begin, I will also make an end. For I have told him that I will judge his house for ever for the iniquity which he knoweth; because his sons made themselves vile, and he restrained them not. <u>***And therefore I have sworn unto the house of Eli, that the iniquity of Eli's house shall not be purged (no atonement or redemption) with sacrifice nor offering forever.***</u>

Consequently, in the day God judged the house of Eli for their iniquity, the sons of Eli died that day. However, a curious thing happened, Eli, upon hearing the news of his sons' death, fell backwards **broke his neck**, and died. So the word is fulfilled – that the donkey (stiff-necked prophet) who is not redeemed should have his neck broken.

Donkey's Jaw And The Prophetic Strong Man

There is yet another picture of the work of the prophet as a *"strong man"* with reference to the donkey. In Genesis 49, Jacob calls the tribe of Dan a judge. There is yet another tribe associated with strength whose deliverer was a prophet sent by God to operate in might. Warriors of the tribe of Dan were called experts at war (1 Chronicles 12).

Samson was from the tribe of Dan, raised a Nazirite, with a prophetic mandate to be a strong-man and deliver Israel from Philistia. The Lord Jesus once said in Mark 3:27; *"No man can enter a strong man's house and spoil his goods, except he will first bind the strong man; and then he will spoil his house"*.

The Philistines came to Judah, spreading themselves around Lehi, to capture Samson. As the story goes in Judges 15, Samson was bound with two new cords and brought to the Philistines. When Samson came to Lehi to meet the Philistines, the Spirit of the Lord came upon him so **mightily** that he broke the cords with which he was bound, found the **jawbone of an ass (donkey)**, and with it slew a thousand men.

There is a dimension of the prophetic where the man of God excels in might! David was a prophet who excelled in might! As the story goes on, Samson became thirsty after his battle, and requested water. Out of the hollow of the jawbone, God caused water to spring forth and refresh his servant.

This is the work of the prophetic – that the jawbone (the mouth and speech) of the prophet will refresh the people of God.

Judges 15:18-19
And he was sore athirst, and called on the LORD, and said, Thou hast given this great deliverance into the hand of thy servant: and now shall I die for thirst, and fall into the hand of the uncircumcised? <u>But God clave an hollow place that was in the jaw</u>, and there came water thereout; and when he had drunk, his spirit came again, and he revived: wherefore he called the name thereof Enhakkore, which is in Lehi unto this day.

Enhakkore means *"fountain of him that called or prayed"*. The jaw of the prophet is a place of strength. This is why the prophet of God is not to be bridled. The jaw is the tool of his trade, and the weapon of his warfare. For this reason, God will promise to guide by his eye, and will counsel his people not to be like a mule which needs a bit and a bridle to be directed (Psalm 32:8-9). A true prophet is completely yielded, and does not need a bridle to be led by God. He is free in God and speaks as God speaks.

The mule is the result of breeding between the horse and the donkey. The horse excels in strength, and does not turn back for fear in the day of battle. The donkey excels in endurance and is wise. The mule possesses the strengths and the qualities of both the horse and the donkey.

The kings of Israel like David and Solomon rode on a mule. On the day of his coronation, Solomon was made to ride on King David's mule. Solomon, as a prophet, came to possess the wisdom and endurance associated with the donkey. Yet Solomon maintained the strength and resolve of a horse, during his reign over Israel. As the mule is sterile and cannot be reproduced, there has arisen no man or prophet in the mold of King Solomon.

The Donkey And The Prophet (Messiah)

In the New Testament, we see a picture of the donkey's prophetic symbolism as it was manifested in the Old Testament. On Palm Sunday, the Lord Jesus Christ rode into Jerusalem on a donkey. Zechariah prophesied that the Messiah would come to Jerusalem, humble and meek, riding on a donkey (Zechariah 9:9). On the day that this picture was played out, the people correctly identified the prophetic office of the Lord Jesus Christ. He was the one whom Moses spoke about saying; *"The LORD thy God will raise up unto thee a Prophet from the midst of thee, of thy brethren, like unto me; unto him ye shall hearken"* (Deuteronomy 18:15). On the day that the Lord Jesus rode into Jerusalem on the donkey, they called him a Prophet!

Matthew 21:9-11
And the multitudes that went before, and that followed, cried, saying, Hosanna to the son of David: Blessed is he that cometh in the name of the Lord; Hosanna in the highest. And when he was come into Jerusalem, all the city was moved, saying, Who is this? And the multitude said, <u>This is Jesus the prophet</u> of Nazareth of Galilee.

Indeed, the Lord Jesus is the Messiah, the Apostle and High Priest of our confession. He is also, the Prophet of God. Indeed He bore God's burden, He bore our sins on the cross and He paid it all.

On the day of the Lord, He will return, this time riding on the horse, because those days will be the days of His power. As the scriptures say in Psalms 110, in the day of His power, His people shall be willing!

Donkey's Prophetic Signature
Chiz C. Chikwendu
© *2011*

King-Priests Releasing The Awesome Power Of God

Did you know that you have a holy calling to be a king and priest unto the Lord? Yes, by the Blood of Jesus you have been made a king and priest and all creation is waiting for you to fulfill this holy calling! You have come to the kingdom for such a time as this to become one of the manifested sons of God! The mysteries revealed in this book are divine strategies from the throne of God to propel you into your final destiny as a king-priest and to manifest the Glory of God!

We are in the last of the last days. As we enter this season, we must enter into a new dimension of prayer. You will begin to understand the powerful connection between your royal priesthood, the Tabernacle of Moses, and the Lord's Prayer Model. Most importantly, it will fulfill the desire of the Lord's heart to bring the Body of Christ into a corporate unity for the end-time harvest of souls and the glorification of the Saints.

In addition to this version, there is the summarized version; *"King-Priests Releasing the Power of Prayer"* and the new workbook format; *"The Awesome Power of God Study Guide"*. You will be forever changed after being enveloped in the pages of these books. They are practical and insightful step-by-step books to teach you who you are and how to manifest *"The Awesome Power of God"* anywhere and at anytime!

For more in-depth information regarding your royal priesthood and how to pray according to the Pattern order:

King-Priests
Releasing
"The Awesome Power Of God"

Visit web site: www.myholycall.com
Email: prayer@myholycall.com

For a summarized version of how to fulfill Your king-priest ministry see the companion booklet!

King-Priests
Releasing
"The Power Of Prayer"

Visit web site: www.myholycall.com
Email: prayer@myholycall.com

The new workbook format for teaching and learning how to fulfill your royal priesthood!

"The Awesome Power of God" Study Guide

Visit web site: www.myholycall.com
Email: prayer@myholycall.com

The Lord called C.J. to enter His presence, know His heart, and share His heart with others. Her book of poetry is an inspiring collection of comforting and uplifting Christian poems. They are designed to glorify our Lord and Savior Jesus Christ and to inspire others to allow His anointed Word to change their lives. You will know the heart of God as you determine to spend time, *"In The KING'S Presence!"*

"In The KING'S Presence"

Visit web site: www.myholycall.com
Email: prayer@myholycall.com

Made in the USA
Charleston, SC
04 September 2011